MUMMY DOGS

and Other HORRIFYING SNACKS

Ali Vega

Lerner Publications ◆ Minneapolis

Lerner Publications Company
A division of Lerner Publishing Group, Inc.
241 First Avenue North
Minneapolis, MN 55401 USA

For reading levels and more information, look up this title at www.lernerbooks.com.

Main body text set in Tw Cen MT Std.
Typeface provided by Monotype.

Library of Congress Cataloging-in-Publication Data

Names: Vega, Ali, author.
Title: Mummy dogs and other horrifying snacks / by Ali Vega.
Description: Minneapolis : Lerner Publications, [2017] | Series: Little kitchen of horrors | Includes bibliographical references and index. | Audience: Age: 7-11.
Identifiers: LCCN 2016019845 (print) | LCCN 2016024263 (ebook) | ISBN 9781512425758 (library bound : alk. paper) | ISBN 9781512428063 (eb pdf)
Subjects: LCSH: Snack foods--Juvenile literature. | Food craft--Juvenile literature. | Cooking--Juvenile literature. | LCGFT: Cookbooks.
Classification: LCC TX740 .V44 2017 (print) | LCC TX740 (ebook) | DDC 641.5/3--dc23

LC record available at https://lccn.loc.gov/2016019845

Manufactured in the United States of America
1-41343-23287-9/2/2016

Photo Acknowledgments
The images in this book are used with the permission of: © Axel Alvarez/ Shutterstock Images, p. 4; © Mighty Media, Inc., pp. 5 (top left), 5 (top right), 5 (bottom), 9 (left), 9 (right), 10, 11 (top), 11 (middle), 11 (bottom), 12, 13 (top), 13 (middle), 13 (bottom), 14, 15 (top), 15 (middle), 15 (bottom), 16, 17 (top), 17 (middle), 17 (bottom), 18, 19 (top), 19 (middle), 19 (bottom), 20, 21 (top), 21 (middle), 21 (bottom), 22, 23 (top), 23 (middle), 23 (bottom), 24, 25 (top), 25 (middle), 25 (bottom), 27 (top), 27 (middle), 27 (bottom), 28, 29 (top), 29 (middle), 29 (bottom); © Elena Elisseeva/Shutterstock Images, p. 6; © photobyphotoboy/Shutterstock Images, p. 7; © Lapina/Shutterstock Images, p. 8; © lightwavemedia/Shutterstock Images, p. 30.

Front Cover: © Mighty Media, Inc.

CONTENTS

Introduction: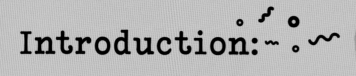

SiCKENING SNACKS

Most kids reach for a snack as soon as they get home from school. What is your go-to treat? Maybe you grab a handful of pretzels and wash them down with a tall glass of juice. Or maybe you nibble on some fruit. But what if those pretzels were covered in snot? Imagine that your juice was made of slime. Picture fruit full of fangs. These dishes may sound horrible. But you're actually in for a delicious treat!

Many people have fun being horrified by food. From nasty booger sticks to spooky cake eyeballs, recipes that look terrible but taste terrific are tons of fun to make and serve. So scour the cupboards, and get ready to make some delightfully disgusting snacks!

Before You
GeT STaRTeD

Cook Safely! Creating stomach-churning snacks means using many different kitchen tools and appliances. These items can be very hot or sharp. Make sure to get an adult's help whenever making a recipe that requires use of an oven, stove, or knife.

Be a Smart Chef! Cooking gross snacks can be messy. Ask an adult for permission before starting a new cooking project. Then make sure you have a clean workspace. Wash your hands often while cooking. If you have long hair, be sure to tie it back. Make sure your guests don't have any food allergies before cooking. Adjust the recipes if you need to. Make sure your disgusting snacks are safe to eat!

Tools You'll Need

Cooking can involve special tools and appliances. You will need the following items for these disgusting recipes:

- microwave
- mixer or hand mixer
- oven
- refrigerator
- stove or hot plate

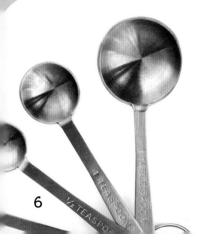

6

METRIC CONVERSION CHART

Use this handy chart to convert recipes to the metric system. If you can't find the conversion you need, ask an adult to help you find an online calculator!

STANDARD	METRIC
¼ teaspoon	1.2 milliliters
½ teaspoon	2.5 ml
¾ teaspoon	3.7 ml
1 teaspoon	5 ml
2 teaspoons	10 ml
1 tablespoon	15 ml
¼ cup	59 ml
⅓ cup	79 ml
½ cup	118 ml
⅔ cup	158 ml
¾ cup	177 ml
1 cup	237 ml

150 degrees Fahrenheit	66 degrees Celsius
300°F	149°C
350°F	177°C
400°F	204°C

1 ounce	28 grams
1 fluid ounce	30 milliliters
1 inch	2.5 centimeters
1 pound	0.5 kilograms

MAKING SNACKS SUPER GROSS

Nasty Names

One trick to making snacks seem gross is to give them nasty names. A sick-sounding title can turn an everyday **edible** into something downright disgusting. Once dishes are given nauseating names, it's hard to imagine them as anything else! Breadsticks become bony fingers. Syrup turns into slime. And kale is crusty skin!

Examine your ingredients as you make your snacks. Do any inspire you to give them nasty names? Make sure to share the terrible title of each dish you serve with your snackers. Their looks of horror are part of the fun!

Sick Snack Setups

Giving food gross names is only part of what makes horrifying snacks scary. The way you serve them is important too. Present your dishes with fun props to make them seem extra spooky. Place a box of facial tissues alongside booger pretzels. Fake bugs and bandages can also grossify your dishes. Make sure to **sanitize** props before using them. And remove the props from the food before serving it to your guests. Keep things fun and delicious without putting your diners in danger.

MUMMY CAKES

These mini mummy pizzas will put a curse on your guests' taste buds!

Ingredients

10–12 black olives
10–12 string cheese sticks
5 cherry tomatoes
10 rice cakes
¾ cup pizza sauce

Tools

• knife
• cutting board
• 2 baking sheets
• measuring cup
• measuring spoons
• oven mitts

Serves: 8–10
Preparation Time: 10–15 minutes

2

1. **Preheat** the oven to 350°F. Cut the olives into round slices. These will be your mummies' eyes.

2. Pull the string cheese apart into thin strands. Cut the cherry tomatoes in half.

3. Place the rice cakes on the baking sheets. Spread 1 tablespoon of pizza sauce on each cake.

4

4. Put two olive eyes on each rice cake. Add a cherry tomato mouth beneath the eyes.

5. Now cover each cake in cheese strands. Arrange them so they look like bandages.

6. With an adult's help, bake the cakes for 3 to 5 minutes. Remove, and let them cool. Your guests will be spooked as they bite into their mini mummies!

5

BOOGER STICKS

No tissues needed for these supersticky booger bites.

Ingredients

3 tablespoons cream cheese
3 tablespoons grated parmesan
    cheese
green food coloring
30–40 pretzel sticks

Tools

• baking sheet
• waxed paper
• measuring spoons
• microwave-safe bowl
• oven mitts
• rubber spatula

Serves: 4–6
Preparation Time: 30–45 minutes

3

1 Cover a baking sheet with waxed paper.

2 Place the cream cheese in a bowl, and microwave on high for 30 seconds. Continue to heat for 15 seconds at a time, stirring between heatings, until the cream cheese is melted and gooey.

3 Carefully remove the bowl from the microwave and add the parmesan cheese. Stir the mixture together with a rubber spatula.

4

4 Stir 3 drops of food coloring into the cheese mixture. It should be a nice booger-green color. Add more food coloring if needed.

5 Dip a pretzel stick in the cheese mixture. Lift it out, and let it cool for 10 seconds. Dip the pretzel stick again, swirl it in the mixture, and lift it out again. Repeat until the cheese mixture looks like a booger on the pretzel. Then set the pretzel on the baking sheet.

6 Repeat step 5 until all the pretzel sticks are coated. Refrigerate the sticks for 10 minutes. Your boogers are ready to serve!

5

CROOKED FiNGER BREAD

These twisted breadsticks look just like crooked, bloody fingers with bright-red nails!

Ingredients

cooking spray
½ red pepper
½ cup (1 stick) unsalted butter
½ teaspoon salt
1 11-ounce tube refrigerated
    breadsticks
½ cup marinara sauce

Tools

- baking sheet
- knife
- cutting board
- measuring cups
- measuring spoons
- small microwave-safe bowl
- oven mitts
- fork
- pastry brush

Serves: 5–6
Preparation Time: 30 minutes

1. Preheat the oven according to the breadsticks package instructions. Lightly coat a baking sheet with cooking spray.

2. Cut the pepper into small triangles. They should look like fingernails.

3. Use the microwave to melt the butter in a small bowl. Then **whisk** in the salt using a fork.

2

4. Pull the breadstick dough apart into individual breadsticks. Then twist each breadstick to look like a crooked finger. Form a big bump in the center of each breadstick to look like a knuckle. Arrange the breadsticks on the baking sheet. Then brush each breadstick lightly with the melted butter and salt mixture.

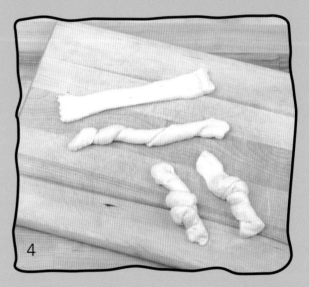

5. Press a pepper slice onto one tip of each breadstick to look like a fingernail.

6. With an adult's help, bake the breadsticks according to the package directions. Then remove them from the oven, and decorate your fingers with marinara sauce to look like blood. Present these bloodstained fingers to your guests, and warn them to watch out for knuckles!

4

5

SLIME COCKTAIL

This sewer-worthy drink may look disgusting. But it's just right for washing down salty snacks.

Ingredients

2 cups pineapple juice
2 cups white grape juice
neon green food coloring
neon blue food coloring
1 can club soda
¼ cup maple syrup

Tools

• measuring cups
• pitcher
• long-handled spoon
• shallow bowl
• mixing spoon
• 6 drinking glasses

Serves: 6
Preparation Time: 10 minutes

1. Pour the pineapple juice and grape juice into a pitcher and stir together.

2. Stir in 10 to 15 drops of neon green food coloring and 4 to 6 drops of neon blue food coloring. The liquid should be a slime-green color. Add more food coloring as needed to get the color you want.

3. Add the club soda to the pitcher, and set it aside.

4. Pour the maple syrup into a shallow bowl. Add 3 drops neon green food coloring and 1 drop of neon blue food coloring. Stir together.

5. Dip the rims of six drinking glasses in the syrup. Then fill them with the juice and soda mixture. Watch your guests try not to gag as they slurp down this tasty cocktail.

2

4

5

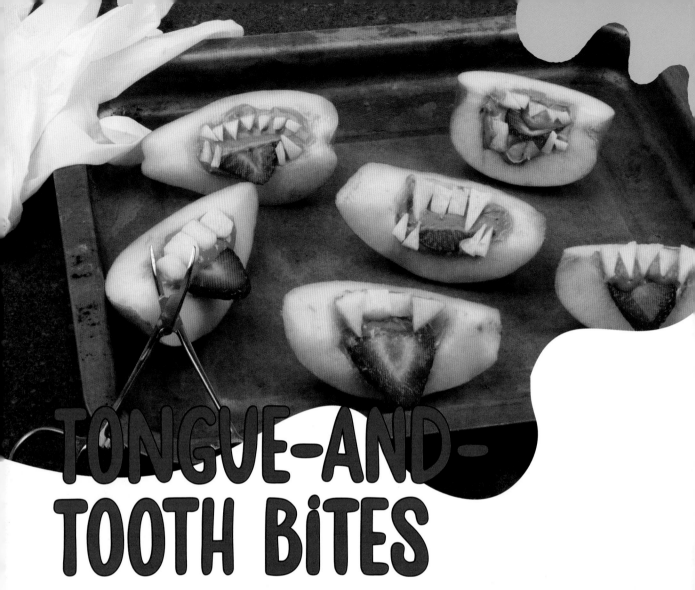

TONGUE-AND-TOOTH BITES

Chomp up these tasty bite-sized fruit pieces before they take a bite out of you!

Ingredients

2 green apples
2 pears
1 **jicama**
5 strawberries
⅓ cup peanut butter

Tools

- knife
- cutting board
- spoon
- peeler
- measuring cups
- table knife

Serves: 4–6
Preparation Time: 15–20 minutes

1. Cut the apples and pears into quarters. Cut the core and seeds out of each fruit piece.

2. Turn each fruit piece so the skin is facing out. Use a spoon to scoop out a mouth-shaped hole.

3. Peel the jicama, and slice it into long strips with an adult's help. Then cut the strips into small, tooth-sized pieces.

4. Remove the strawberry stems. Slice each berry lengthwise into four to six pieces.

5. Spread peanut butter inside each fruit piece's hole.

6. Stick the jicama pieces into the peanut butter to look like teeth. Then add a strawberry-slice tongue to each piece of fruit. Your toothy fruit bites are ready for snacking!

1

2

3

TIP

If one of your guests has a peanut allergy, use sunflower butter instead of peanut butter. This creamy spread is made from sunflower seeds.

CHARRED ZOMBIE-SKIN CRISPS

Crispy zombie skin makes a healthful treat.

Ingredients

Barbecue Sauce

1 cup ketchup

¼ cup apple cider vinegar

1 tablespoon honey

1 tablespoon brown sugar

1¼ teaspoons paprika

1¼ teaspoons garlic powder

1 tablespoon Worcestershire sauce

2 bunches kale

Tools

- measuring cups
- measuring spoons
- saucepan
- mixing spoon
- baking sheet
- parchment paper
- dish towel or paper towel
- knife
- cutting board
- pastry brush
- oven mitts
- tongs
- small bowl for serving

Serves: 4–6
Preparation Time: 1½ hours

1. Stir the barbecue sauce ingredients together in a saucepan. With an adult's help, bring the sauce to a **simmer** over medium heat. Then turn the heat to low and cook for 1 hour, stirring every 10 minutes. Remove the sauce from heat and set aside.

2. Preheat the oven to 350°F. Cover a baking sheet with parchment paper.

3. Wash the kale and pat it dry with a dish towel or paper towel. Cut out the stems, and chop the leaves into smaller pieces.

4. Spread out the kale leaves on the baking sheet. Brush each leaf with a small amount of barbecue sauce.

5. Bake the kale for 10 minutes. Use tongs to turn the leaves over and bake for another 10 to 15 minutes.

6. Remove the baking sheet from the oven, and serve the kale with a small bowl of barbecue sauce. These crispy greens may look undead, but they will be gone before you know it!

1

3

4

TIP

Speed up this recipe by using premade barbecue sauce.

POPPED BRAINS

These brains are oh-so-sweet and extra crunchy for a mind-bending treat!

Ingredients

5 tablespoons butter

1 10.5-ounce package marshmallows

1 tablespoon vanilla extract

red food coloring

¼ cup chopped walnuts

6–8 cups popped and lightly salted popcorn

½ cup white chocolate chips

¼ cup raspberry jam

Tools

- measuring spoons
- large stockpot
- baking sheet
- waxed paper
- measuring cups
- mixing spoon
- table knife

Serves: 8
Preparation Time: 15–20 minutes

1. Melt the butter in a stockpot over low heat. Cover a baking sheet with waxed paper.

2. Add the marshmallows to the stockpot, and stir until they melt. Then add the vanilla extract and 3 drops of food coloring.

3. Stir in the walnuts. Then pour in the popcorn, and stir until it is coated with the marshmallow mixture. Stir in the white chocolate chips until they melt. Remove the stockpot from heat, and allow the mixture to cool until it is safe to work with but still warm.

3

4. With clean hands, form the popcorn mixture into eight balls of equal size. Place them on the baking sheet.

5. Next gently form each ball into a brain shape. Make a slight dent down the center of each ball to look like a brain.

6. Use a table knife to put a line of raspberry jam down each brain's dent. These brainy bites are ready to make your snackers smarter!

5

TIP

Latex-free gloves can help keep your hands clean while forming these sticky brains.

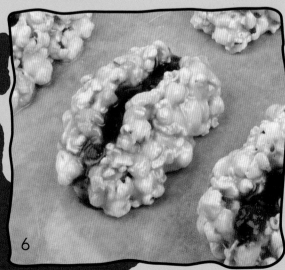

6

MUMMY DOGS

These spooky little mummies look like they came straight out of the tomb!

Ingredients

2 tablespoons mayonnaise
1 teaspoon mustard
2 black olives
1 11-ounce package refrigerated
   breadstick dough
8 hot dogs
ketchup, for serving

Tools

• measuring spoons
• small bowl
• mixing spoon
• knife
• cutting board
• baking sheet
• oven mitts
• toothpick

Serves: 6–8
Preparation Time: 25 minutes

1. Preheat the oven to 375°F. Stir together the mayonnaise and mustard in a small bowl. Chop the olives into tiny pieces. These will be your mummies' eyes.

2. Remove the breadstick dough from the package and pull apart into individual breadsticks. Stretch out each breadstick with your hands until it is long and skinny.

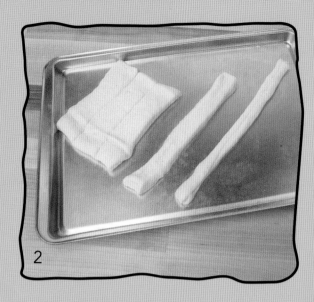

2

3. Wrap each hot dog in one piece of breadstick dough. The dough should look like a mummy's bandages. Arrange the dough-wrapped hot dogs on the baking sheet. Bake for 15 to 18 minutes, or until golden brown.

4. Remove the baking sheet from the oven, and let the hot dogs cool. Use a toothpick to add two drops of the mayonnaise-mustard mixture to each hot dog. These should look like eyes. Then add an olive-piece pupil to each drop.

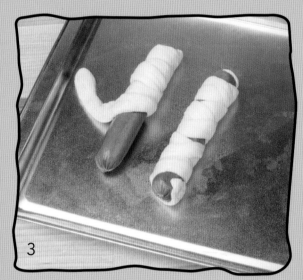

3

5. Serve your mini mummies with a bit of ketchup to satisfy hungry snackers!

TIP

These monstrous mummies can also be made from turkey dogs or vegetarian hot dogs!

4

SWEET CAKE EYEBALLS

These supersweet eyeballs make a perfect snack to stare right back.

Ingredients

Cake
cooking spray
1 16.5-ounce box red velvet cake mix
⅓ cup vegetable oil (or amount on cake mix package)
3 large eggs (or amount on cake mix package)

Frosting
½ cup (1 stick) butter, softened
1 8-ounce package cream cheese
1 tablespoon vanilla extract
4 cups powdered sugar

Candy Coating
2 16-ounce packages white chocolate candy coating
20–30 small round coated chocolate candy pieces
red and black writing gel

Tools

- 1 13 x 9-inch cake pan
- measuring spoons
- measuring cups
- mixing bowls
- mixing spoons
- oven mitts
- wire cooling rack
- mixer or hand mixer
- 2 baking sheets
- waxed paper
- toothpick
- serving plate

Serves: 10–20
Preparation Time: 4–5 hours

1. Preheat the oven according to the cake mix package instructions. Lightly coat the cake pan with cooking spray.

2. Stir the cake ingredients together in a mixing bowls. Pour the **batter** into the cake pan, and bake according to the package instructions. Turn the cake out onto a wire rack to cool.

3

3. While the cake is cooling, make the frosting. Put the butter, cream cheese, and vanilla in a mixing bowl. Beat with a mixer on low speed. Add the powdered sugar 1 cup at a time, and beat until creamy.

4. Cover two baking sheets with waxed paper.

5. With clean hands, crumble the cake into a large bowl. Add 2 cups of frosting. Mix together with your hands.

5

6. With clean hands, form small round balls from the cake and frosting mixture. Each should be about the size of a golf ball. Put the cake balls on the baking sheet. Refrigerate them for 2 hours.

TIP

To tell if your cake is done cooking, insert a toothpick or table knife into the cake's center. If the toothpick or knife comes out clean, the cake is fully cooked!

6

Sweet Cake Eyeballs continued next page

TIP

Writing gel is a type of frosting that is perfect for creating piping or writing on desserts. It is available at most grocery stores or online.

Sweet Cake Eyeballs, continued

7 When your cake balls are chilled, it's time to make the coating. Microwave the white chocolate candy coating on low power for 1 minute. Stir the coating for a few seconds. Then microwave for 30 more seconds, and stir again. Continue cooking for 30 seconds and stirring until the coating is melted.

8

8 Gently drop a cake ball in the candy coating. Use a spoon to roll the ball around in the coating until it is completely covered.

9 Place the coated cake ball back on the baking sheet. Press a candy piece in the center of the ball. The cake ball should look like an eyeball with an iris.

10

10 Repeat steps 8 and 9 with the remaining cake balls. Then refrigerate them for 15 more minutes.

11 Use the red writing gel to add veins to each eyeball.

12 Put a black dot of the writing gel in the center of each candy piece to look like a pupil. Arrange these spooky snacks on a serving plate, where they can glare at hungry guests!

11

WRAPPING UP

Cleaning Up

Once you are done cooking, it is time to clean up! Make sure to wipe up spills, wash dishes, and clear the table. Wash and put away any props you used that don't belong in the kitchen. Make sure any leftovers are properly packaged and refrigerated.

Keep Cooking!

Let the revolting snack recipes you made inspire you! Think of ways to put your own terrifying twists to the recipes you tried. Or dream up your own disgusting snack ideas. Think gross, and keep on cooking!

GLOSSARY

batter: a thin mixture containing flour, eggs, oil, or other ingredients that is used to make baked goods

edible: something that can be safely eaten

jicama: a starchy root vegetable native to Mexico that can be eaten cooked or raw

latex: a substance used to make some rubber products

preheat: to heat an oven to the required temperature before putting in the food

sanitize: to clean something so it is free of germs

simmer: when a heated liquid is not quite boiling and has very small bubbles

vegetarian: without meat

whisk: to stir very quickly using a fork or a tool made of curved wire, also called a whisk

FURTHER INFORMATION

Cornell, Kari A. *Awesome Snacks and Appetizers.* Minneapolis: Millbrook Press, 2014.
Put your own spooky spin on these simple snack recipes.

Kids' Snack Recipes
http://allrecipes.com/recipes/1659/appetizers-and-snacks/snacks/kids
Check out these fun and easy recipes perfect for an after-school treat or the next time you have friends over.

Mills, Jill. *Wild Eats and Adorable Treats: 40 Animal-Inspired Meals and Snacks for Kids.* New York: Skyhorse Publishing, 2015.
Discover how to create snacks and other foods shaped like your favorite animals with this fun cookbook.

10 Healthy Halloween Treats for Kids
http://www.everydayhealth.com/healthy-halloween-treats-for-kids.aspx
These healthful and spooky snacks are as fun to make as they are to eat.

INDEX